SEA FAN OR GORGONIAN

Animals that Live in the Sea

By Joan Ann Straker

An octopus uses its eight arms to crawl on the ocean floor.

☐ BOOKS FOR YOUNG EXPLORERS
NATIONAL GEOGRAPHIC SOCIETY

The sea is a home for many different kinds of animals.

There is a strange
and beautiful world
in the waters of the sea.
It is full of creatures very different
from the animals that live on land.

Imagine you are deep in the ocean.
You can see fishes in bright colors.
You may find a yellow sea slug
and a starfish with five arms.
There are also many other animals
that you have never seen before.

SEA SLUG OR NUDIBRANCH

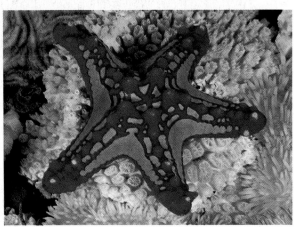

KNOBBED STARFISH

There are many kinds of fishes.

Fishes have many shapes and sizes.
Some are so strange that you might think they are not fish.

SEA HORSE

BUTTERFLY FISH

Yellow and black stripes
make this fish
as bright as a butterfly.

Sea horses are the only fish
that use their tails
to hold onto things underwater.

A goosefish lies flat as a pancake on the bottom of the ocean.

GOOSEFISH

A lumpy frogfish looks like an orange blob in the sea.

BLUE SHARK

STINGRAY

MANTA RAY

Sharks and rays are fishes, too.

The blue shark is a very good hunter.
It swims so fast it almost always catches the fish it chases.

Rays are fish with very flat bodies.
The spotted stingray has fins that circle its body.
It wiggles them as it swims.
The huge manta ray has large fins that look like wings.
It also has smaller fins on the sides of its mouth.

Some animals
are fast swimmers.

YELLOWFIN TUNA

Tuna are among
the fastest fishes
in the sea.
The shape of their
long, smooth bodies
helps them
speed along.

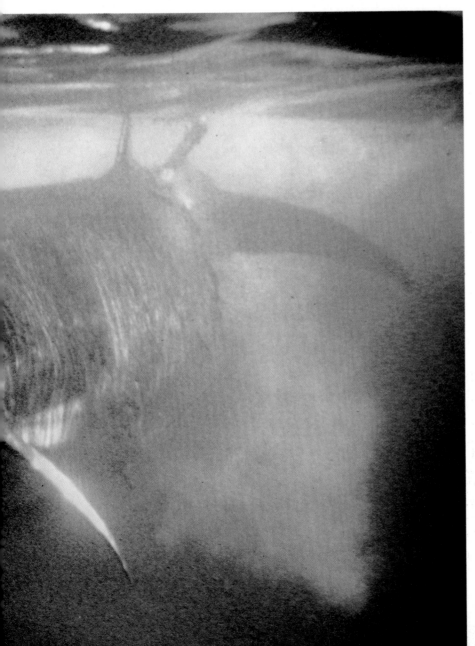

This mighty whale is
a large and heavy mammal.
It also has
a long, smooth body
and can move easily
through the water.

SEI WHALE

PORTUGUESE
MAN-OF-WAR

These animals float in the sea.

A Portuguese man-of-war floats in the water like a purple balloon. It will eat the fish it has caught in its long tentacles.

The starfish floats when it is young and has a tail. When the starfish is grown, it loses its tail and lives on the bottom of the sea.

The striped jellyfish moves slowly in the water by opening and closing its umbrella top.

STARFISH LARVA

STRIPED JELLYFISH

Some animals hardly move at all.

These strawberry sponges look like vases.
Sponges stay in one spot most of their lives
and feed on the tiny plants that float in the sea.

The yellow sea pen is an animal that looks like a feather.
It buries its stem in the mud to hold its place on the seafloor.

STRAWBERRY SPONGES

SEA PEN

Sea anemones are animals that look like flowers.
A hungry sea anemone has opened its tentacles to catch food.
The other closes them to eat what it has caught.

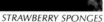

WHITE-SPOTTED SEA ANEMONES

There are many kinds of coral.

SEA FAN

BUBBLE CORAL

In some places in the sea, there are groups of animals
that look like plants or rocks. These animals are called corals.
Corals have many different shapes and colors.
Can you guess why the purple coral is called a sea fan?
Look closely at the yellow coral and you will find a starfish.

PRECIOUS CORAL

This piece of bright coral looks like a tree branch.
Many small coral creatures live there.
These animals stretch out their white tentacles to feed.

Many fishes live among the corals.

Corals create places in the sea called coral reefs.
There many fishes hide and find their food.
A parrotfish scrapes small plants and animals off the coral with its strong, sharp teeth.

PARROTFISH

Parrotfish have large teeth that show all the time. So these fish always seem to be smiling.

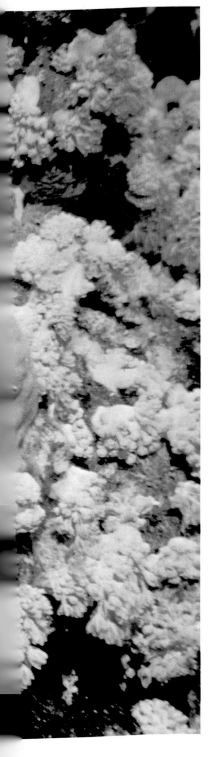

PARROTFISH

The long-nosed hawkfish matches the colors of the coral where it lives.

HAWKFISH

GARIBALDI AND STARFISH

These animals are defending their homes.

Two lobsters are fighting
with their claws.
One lobster has knocked
the other over on its side.
They will fight to the death.
A lobster will attack an animal
that comes near its home.

An orange garibaldi protects its home, too.
When a starfish comes near,
the garibaldi picks it up
and moves it away.

SCALLOPS   STARFISH

A hungry starfish has caught a scallop. The starfish pulls and pulls.
It is trying to pull the scallop's shells apart to eat the animal inside.
The other scallops speed away as fast as they can.
Scallops move by opening their shells and snapping them together.

One animal
becomes food for another.

SEA ANEMONE AND STARFISH

In another part of the ocean, a sea anemone has caught a starfish.
The anemone stings the starfish so it cannot move.
The anemone pulls the starfish into its mouth.
Do you see the starfish in the tentacles of the anemone?

21

These fish swim together for safety.

These goatfish live and swim together in a group. A group of the same kind of fish is called a school.

If a hungry animal swims near so many fish,
it may become confused and not be able to pick out a single one.
Many fish spend most of their lives in the same school.

These fishes are hiding in safe places.

A school of little blue fish swims among branches of coral. They are safe there because bigger fish cannot follow them.

A small pearlfish lives inside a gray sea cucumber. It wiggles out to hunt for food.

This blenny is a tiny fish
with big eyes.
It peeks out of a tube
it has found.
The tube was built by a sea worm.

DAMSELFISH

BLENNY

SEA CUCUMBER
AND
PEARLFISH

A few sea animals use poison for protection.

SEA SNAKE

With its tail floating high,
a sea snake pokes its head into the sand
to look for fish eggs.
Animals do not attack this sea snake.
Perhaps they know
it has a very deadly poison.

The stonefish lies on the sea bottom
looking as flat and harmless as a stone.
But spines hidden on its back
contain a very strong poison.

STONEFISH

The striped lionfish has long fins
that look like ribbons. The fish is no longer
than your foot, but it is poisonous, too.

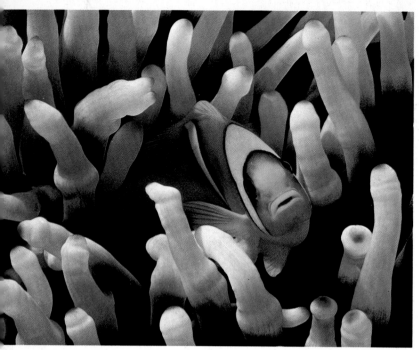

CLOWNFISH

Some sea animals help each other.

The tentacles of a sea anemone
protect the little clownfish.
When the clownfish is attacked,
it rushes to the anemone for safety.
If the attacker gets too close,
the anemone stings and kills it.
And both animals have
something to eat.

Two sea anemones ride
on a crab's shell.
They cover the shell
and make the crab harder to see.
When the crab catches food,
the anemones eat the leftovers.

HERMIT CRAB AND SEA ANEMONES

**How very different
are the animals
that live in the sea!**

Dolphins surf
in big ocean waves.
The red feather star
usually stays in one place.
The sea turtle paddles
through the water
with its flippers,
and the crab walks sideways
on its eight legs.

FEATHER STAR

HAWKSBILL TURTLE

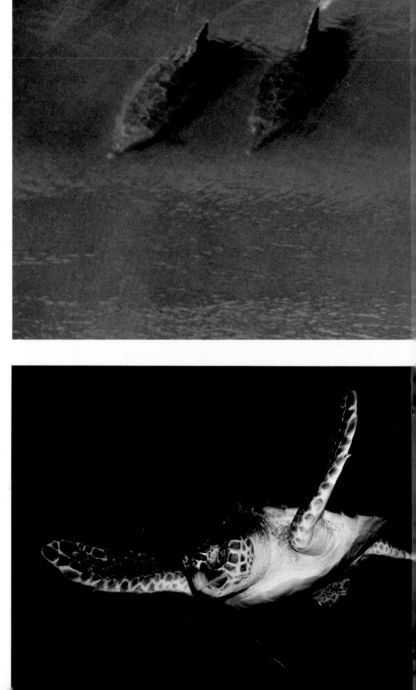

BOTTLENOSED DOLPHINS

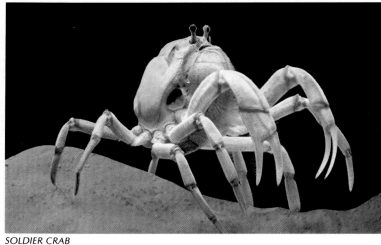

SOLDIER CRAB

There are many other animals
in the strange and beautiful
ocean world.
Each kind has
its own way of living
in the waters of the sea.

A wolffish hides
in a space between two rocks.

Published by The National Geographic Society
Robert E. Doyle, *President;* Melvin M. Payne, *Chairman of the Board;*
Gilbert M. Grosvenor, *Editor;* Melville Bell Grosvenor, *Editor Emeritus*

Prepared by
The Special Publications Division
Robert L. Breeden, *Editor*
Donald J. Crump, *Associate Editor*
Philip B. Silcott, *Senior Editor*
Cynthia Russ Ramsay, *Managing Editor*
Elizabeth W. Fisher, *Researcher*
Jane Clarke, *Communications Research Assistant*

Illustrations
Geraldine Linder, *Picture Editor*
Suez B. Kehl, *Art Director*

Production and Printing
Robert W. Messer, *Production Manager*
George V. White, *Assistant Production Manager*
Raja D. Murshed, June L. Graham, Christine A. Roberts, David V. Showers, *Production Assistants*
Debra A. Antonini, Barbara Bricks, Jane H. Buxton, Suzanne J. Jacobson, Katheryn M. Slocum, Suzanne Venino, *Staff Assistants*

Consultants
Dr. Glenn O. Blough, Peter L. Munroe, *Educational Consultants*
Edith K. Chasnov, *Reading Consultant*
Dr. Victor G. Springer, Smithsonian Institution, *Scientific Consultant*

Illustrations Credits
D. P. Wilson, F.R.P.S. (1, 11 top); Valerie Taylor (2 top); Dr. E. R. Degginger, APSA (2 bottom, 27); David Doubilet (2-3, 6 bottom left, 15 top right, 17 bottom, 18-19, 22-23, 24-25, 26 right, 28); Aldo Margiocco (4 top left); Dr. Giuseppe Mazza (4 top right, 15 bottom, 28-29, 31 bottom); Douglas Faulkner (4 bottom); Carl Roessler (5, 30 top left); Howard Hall (6-7 top); Ron and Valerie Taylor (6-7 bottom); William L. High (8-9 top); Gordon R. Williamson, Bruce Coleman Inc. (8-9 bottom); Runk/Schoenberger, Grant Heilman (10); Ron Church (11 bottom); Peter D. Capen, Terra Mar Productions (12 left); Neil G. McDaniel (12 right, 13, 32); Eva Cropp (14); Thomas Cowell (15 top left); Raymond F. Hixon (16-17); W. A. Starck II (17 top); Richard Murphy/After Image (19); Robert F. Sisson, National Geographic Natural Science Photographer (20-21); John Boland, Sea Library (21); Stephen Spotte (25 top); Jen and Des Bartlett (25 bottom); Ben Cropp (26 left); Bruce Coleman Inc. (30 bottom right); Scott Preiss (30-31 top).

Cover Photograph: Stan Keiser, Sea Library
Endpaper Photograph: David Doubilet

Library of Congress CIP Data
Straker, Joan Ann, 1943-   Animals that live in the sea.   (Books for young explorers)
SUMMARY: An introduction to the characteristics and natural environment of a variety
of creatures inhabiting the ocean.
1. Marine fauna—Juvenile literature. [1. Marine animals] I. Title. II. Series.
QL122.2.S8   591.9'2   77-95415   ISBN 0-87044-264-3